CRITICAL SELF-ANALYSIS

The Key to True Happiness in Christ

Transcending the seven
nails of the carnal mind

TEACHER

Alain Yaovi M. Dagba

Introduction

Who are you? How are you doing with yourself? When you think about yourself, what comes into your mind? When you are facing difficult situations, what comes out of you?

In **Genesis 1, 26**, it is written that you and I have been created in the image and the likeness of God. But what does this mean? Do we really feel this and experience this to be true? If not, why?

How is your relationship with yourself? How is your relationship with others? Do you feel fulfilled? Are you happy with your life? What about your past? Do you feel trapped in past pains? What about your future? Are you anxious about what tomorrow may be or look like?

The bible said that, "we are God's handiwork, created in Christ Jesus to do good works, which God prepared in advance for us to do" **(Ephesians 2: 10).**

But why is it that our lives sometimes feel empty and purposeless?

Do you feel sometimes as though life or people are unfair to you? Do you have principles you live by? What are your principles? The truth is, no matter how you feel or what you think about your life and others, the answer is nowhere else but with you.

It is all about you understanding who you are, understanding how your universe functions, and having control of your universe without trying to control others. And this is done through critical self-analysis. This material is a mirror to your soul. It makes you see yourself, and provides for you ways to grow yourself and become a better person full of joy and happiness.

PRIOR TO WRITING THIS BOOK

I could say that this book is the extended and detailed version of the previous course I gave my students on the power of critical self-analysis (CSA).

The first time I taught them on CSA was when I was training them on the subject of leadership. Here I would like to share with you the first lesson on CSA, before you start your study on the extended and detailed version, which is this book.

I have also taught my students on the fourteen nails of the ego or the carnal mind. However, I was not able to complete the teaching with them. As I continued my meditation with the Lord on the nails or grips of the ego, it became clear to me that there are actually only seven nails, and each one of them duplicates its own contents into a specific character.

In this book, I explain the seven nails of the ego, and show how by identifying them during your CSA, you could easily heal yourself from them and become a better person.

MY FIRST TEACHING ON CSA

What is critical self-analysis and what is the benefit?

David prayed: "Search me, God, and know my heart; test me and know my anxious thoughts. See if there is any offensive way in me, and lead me in the way everlasting" **(Psalm 139: 23-24)**.

To conduct a critical self-analysis, one needs to learn to see himself in situations. When an event occurs, one must learn to ask the following questions, not to blame oneself, but to recognize the different data that are working against the voice of inspiration or the Holy Spirit within, which only leads to goodness and well-being. Here are the questions:

- What could I have done better to avoid this situation? Lord show me.

- What is it that I need to change in my character? Lord show me.

- Is there anything I should not have thought, said, and do? Lord show me.

The critical self-analysis allows you to be honest toward yourself, to accept your own criticism and to see yourself for what you are and what you are not.

One always fails to see himself/herself when he or she has the habit to only see others and blame others.

Those who cannot see themselves cannot improve their character. They are always sightless when it comes to their own mistakes. They hate correction; therefore dislike truth.

Proverbs 12: 1 says that "Whoever loves discipline loves knowledge, but whoever hates correction is stupid."

The moment one begins to see his shortcomings, one also comes to transcend negative data programmed in the mind.

Once these negative data are located, accepted, and worked on, one becomes more in touch with the realm of inspiration from within.

With persistent *and* in conducting multiple critical self-analysis, one frees himself /herself from the impulse of negative data, one can exercise control over his thoughts and emotions, direct his thoughts toward better choices and apply his heart to inspirational decisions to produce nothing else but goodness and well-being.

How is the CSA conducted?

David prayed, "Create in me a pure heart, O God, and renew a steadfast spirit within me" **(Psalm 51: 10).**

First, once a negative data is located, one should accept it as being part of one character.

A character is not you. It is like a character in a book or a movie, created by the mind. Your mind is like a stage master. It creates characters to play different movies based on assumptions. But you are not these characters. They are personalities with roles, which you must clear out.

For example, if anger is the negative data, one should have the courage to voice it out: *"I have an anger problem"*.

Second, one should study and see the danger of allowing the negative data (anger) to take control of one's mind and heart. This is a great way to increase the awareness of the issue in one's mind and create for oneself the urgency in wanting to get rid of the negative data.

For instance, until one is educated to see the danger that is in smoking cigarettes, the awareness of the danger of putting nicotine into the body is low, and the desire to stop smoking is almost non-existent.

Therefore, one should study the danger of the negative data. Once the awareness of the danger of that negative data is created, the desire to change becomes real.

Third, one should recount how one feels when the negative data takes over the mind and the heart. *"How do I feel when the data starts manifesting itself or when it takes over my mind, emotions, and actions?"*

I will give you an example.

In the case of anger:

- The heart beats fast (loss of emotional control)

- The mind thinks fast (Loss of mental control)

- The body moves fast (Loss of body control)

- Breathing becomes fast (Risk of Heart attack)

- One is less conscious (Past hurts resurface)

- Negative desires and thoughts arises

- Bad and hurtful decisions are made

- The desire to resent comes into heart

- Hurtful words are spoken

- Physical attacks take place

- Headaches

- Migraine

- Pain in joints (Arthritis)

- Desire to be drunk

- Suicidal and more…

Fourth, after one is aware of his conditions when the negative data takes over, one should make a decision to love oneself enough to let go of the negative data.

Do not deny that you have a negative character. David said to the Lord, "I know my transgression and my sin is always before me" (**Psalm 51: 3**).

If one could not recall how one feels when the negative data emerges, one could read about the negative data in books or search for related documentaries.

If one loves himself enough, one should seek for healing. Most people reject the idea of self-healing.

However, nothing begins without self-healing. You have to make yourself accept your weaknesses. This is self-healing or the removal of the character of arrogance.

God will heal you with your faith. Being able to awake faith in you is self-healing, because doubt is a spiritual illness. The self-healing process begins with learning to observe more than acting.

For instance, when an event is about to trigger the spirit of anger or the negative data, one should become an observer of his own *self* and become conscious of every bit of reactions taking place within. One should make an auto-suggestion in the heat of the moment. This should be done mentally with slow breathing.

An example of auto-suggestion: *"I am witnessing anger (negative data) rising up from within me. I know it is not good for me. I made the decision to only produce good and well-being for myself and others."*

One should repeat the auto-suggestion in perfect silence until the stimulating event stops on its own. The stimulating event is whatever is making you angry.

Right after the auto-suggestion and feeling the result, a certain rushing feeling of joy takes over the soul; for one knows that a victory has been reached.

"Love rejoices with truth" (**1 Corinthians 13: 6**). You have to love yourself enough to admit your mistakes, and joy will be the result.

This joy is from the place of inspiration, the Holy Spirit within. This is the fifth stage of critical self-analysis. However, this fifth stage is not reached until the preliminary stages are completed.

If one has many negative data, they must be confronted one by one.

However, this must be done with a lot of patience.

"Love is patient" **(1 Corinthians 13: 4).** You have to love yourself enough to be patient with yourself.

Usually negative data are connected to each other, and begin to vanish once some are being deleted.

I will add this. If one cannot do the auto-suggestion or speak self-healing words, one should seek for help by calling on a prayer partner.

What have you learned so far?

_____

_____

_____

_____

_____

_____

_____

_____

_____

_____

_____

_____

_____

_____

_____

_____

_____

_____

_____

_____

_____

Part 1

Who are you?

First, I would like to talk to you about *Identity crisis*. I believe I am about to write one of the most significant concept on self-discovery, which the world needs the most. I can feel it. I can feel it. It is also going to be the most helpful note, for anyone who has embarked on the journey of self-discovery.

The mythologist, Joseph Campbell, said something very powerful. I will share with you here what he said. He said, *"The privilege of a lifetime is being who you are"*. Yet, I ask, "How can you be what you do not know?"

Joseph was right. He was right because true happiness and fulfillment start from that privilege to be who you are. I pose you the question. Who are you? Now, pose the question back to yourself. *Who am I*? I mean it. Do it seriously. Close your eyes. Ask yourself the question. *Who am I?* This is a very important thing to do.

Stay with the question for a moment. See if you get any answer. You probably know a lot about other things. However, do you know enough about yourself?

Humans spend a lot of time studying on different subjects. They love to be intellectual. They love to know. They study plants. They study minerals. They study animals. Who is to study you but yourself? No one is closer to you than you are. Sometimes we use religious excuses not to study ourselves.

God has given power to man and woman to subdue sin, from the beginning, even before Jesus came. God told Cain, "in is crouching at the door, eager to control you. But you must subdue it and be its master" (**Genesis 4: 7**).

Who are you? You may be trying to give a meaning to your life right now. However, here is another amazing truth that Joseph ever spoke. He said, *"Life has no meaning. Each of us has meaning and we bring it to life. It is a waste to be asking the question when you are the answer."*

You are the answer to the meaning of your life. Do you have a meaning? What makes you meaningful? Who are you? To know "you" is to touch the face of a supreme Reality or God.

Wisdom is the ability to touch the face of supreme Reality by first standing on logical realities. So, let us look into some logics here. We already know one thing. We know that when we cannot find an answer to the question: *Where am I*, it simply means that we are lost.

Let us suppose that you are journeying through a forest, and at one point you wondered, "Where am I?" This will simply mean that you are lost. Nothing more, and nothing less. Maybe before we find out about who you are, you need to know where you are. Therefore, I will start from there.

Where are you? You could have many answers to this question. You could say, *"I am home reading this note. I am lying down. I am at work. I am so and so."*

You will not be wrong with these answers, because you will be answering a question that you understood.

However, my question is deeper than you seeing yourself in a particular location. Let me help you understand the question with a small story.

In a certain African culture, before they give a woman to a man to wed, the latter will go through a test. In a public setting, the villagers will bring about five or six women dressed alike, of the same height, and the same allure to the groom to be.

They will then cover each woman's face. The man will be asked to recognize his beloved by intuition.

Because the ladies' faces are covered, and outwardly they all look the same, the man could be easily confused, unless he has developed a connection beyond the body and the appearances with his beloved. If not, he will be looking for his beloved, and will not find her behind the covers.

The images we put on to fool others or impress them are fading glories. The bible says that "the Lord sees not as man sees: man looks on the outward appearance, but the Lord looks on the heart" (1 **Samuel 16: 7).**

Are you wearing a mask right now? Is a veil covering your face? Have you covered your face with many identities? Just as the woman is hidden behind a veil from the man, many people are hiding behind many images the society has given them, which they have accepted. In addition, they have created many other images to cover their own face. So, I am asking you again: *Where are you?*

Sometimes the covers are attached so strongly to the face and for so long; that they have difficulties coming off.

Removing them will cause much pain. These people fall into what I call an *identity crisis*. This means, they themselves come to forget how their real face looks like. They do not know if they are the mask, or the face wearing the mask.

This is why when I ask you, *"Where are you"*, you may find some difficulties to answer the question. The truth is you are behind many masks, many images, and many personalities. You are buried so deep underneath them, that even my question was not able to reach your understanding when you first heard it.

I will tell you another story to help you see where I am going with this. In a certain village, a certain boy took his mother's needle and went off to play with his friends in a farmhouse. When he was about to leave the house his mother called him. Afraid that the mother would find out about his behavior, he hid the needle in a haystack. After he was done speaking with his mother, he returned to look for the needle, but could not find it. He started talking to himself: *"Where is this needle hiding?"*

Where are you? Have you gotten lost inside the haystack of many images and personalities? Are you having difficulties finding yourself now that you are returning to look for *"you"*?

Let me tell you a secret; every challenge you face in life is an opportunity to find yourself. If you agree with me that there is nothing more important than *"you"*, don't you think that the pain one goes through to find himself/herself is worth the time and the sacrifice?

How many of *you's* am I speaking to right now? There are three of you. First, the person people think that you are. Second, the person you think that you are and lastly the person that you truly are. The first two constitute the masks, the covers, the images, and the personalities, even if they sound good to keep. Each one of them carries other additional images.

It is painful to remove a mask that has been placed on the face for a very long time. The face with time, takes the shape of the mask. Yet, until your true face returns, happiness could only be a dream. You have a name, but you are not your name. You have a house, but you are not the house. You have money, but you are not the money.

You have children, but you are not your children. You have degrees, but you are not your achievement. You are wise, but you are not your wisdom. You hide yourself underneath all these things. You use them as excuses to hide your real face, because you are afraid to let go of what you are not.

These images can talk and make convincing suggestions to you. They would say, *"If you let us go, you will no longer feel safe; though living you will feel as though you are dying." You are going to die."* Yet, it is within this death that you will find yourself. It is by burning the hay, that the boy will find his needle. Saint Francis would say, *"It is by dying that we will come to eternal life"*. The Christ spoke through Jesus these words, *"If you want to save your life, you will lose it. If you want to lose your life to find me, you will save it"*.

Where are you? Your true SELF, CHRIST, is calling from the deepest part of your soul, *"find me! Find me!"* Are you willing to lose the life these personalities have given you, so that you may find your SELF and live your real LIFE?

Where are you? Are you willing to take off the masks, despite the pain that you know this will cause? Joseph Campbell also said, *"Where you stumble and fall, there you will find gold. The cave you fear to enter holds the treasure you seek."* This cave is within. Jesus called the same cave the "kingdom of God" within. You are nowhere outside to be found. Your true SELF is within this inner cave like a treasure hidden in the field of many personalities.

However, be aware of one thing. The minute you make the decision to take the journey within to find your SELF, the masks will begin to talk and fight back. This could be scary. They will oppose anything that is true and convince you not to take part of it. In addition, because you came to believe that they are who you are, you will also believe whatever they say. You will make of their lies your truth.

Some people stay trapped behind those masks for more than ten years; then after, they made the choice to take the journey of critical self-analysis. Some even die without taking the journey to the glorious castle of their true SELF, which lies deep within the soul. I believe in you. I know you can make it there; if you truly want to.

What have you learned so far?

_____

_____

_____

_____

_____

_____

_____

_____

_____

_____

_____

_____

_____

_____

_____

_____

_____

_____

_____

_____

Part 2

What you are not

What you are not is what most people call the *"ego", the sinful nature, or the carnal mind.* However, what is the ego? I will explain the ego to you, and I want you to read the following lines as a personal letter I have sent to you. Let us start.

You will surely notice that when you want to talk about yourself, your opinion, or voice out a thought, you usually use the word *"I am", "I will", "I want", "I do".*

Paul said, "And if I do what I do not want to do, I agree that the law is good. As it is, it is no longer I myself who do it, but it is sin living in me" (**Romans 7: 16-17**).

Paul is teaching us that what we ARE in reality cannot do what is wrong. However, there is something else in us or someone else in us that can sin. Paul was able to personalize sin as an independent being acting through us, because he understood the ego.

So I was saying that you will surely notice that when you want to talk about yourself, your opinion, or voice out a thought, you usually use the word *"I am"*, *"I will"*, *"I want"*, *"I do"*.

This *"I"* that runs through almost every bit of your expression, is the ego, and there is absolutely nothing wrong with using this "I" to express yourself. I call this *"I"* the basic ego.

The basic ego is an important awareness that gives us a sense of beingness. Without this *"I"* you would not have awareness of yourself and you would not even be able to have consciousness of things.

Therefore, everyone needs this basic ego for survival. All creatures have it. It's the basic ego that is also expressed as:

- "me"
- "myself"
- "mine"

Now, the basic ego could grow to become either a <u>selfish ego</u> or a <u>selfless ego</u>.

These are the only two options the ego really has. There are no others. I will tell you exactly how it happens.

This basic ego in a child is what we call innocence. Innocence here means absence of differences in consciousness and absence of the awareness of separation. Everything is ONE.

As the child is growing, he/she begins to notice the difference between his/her parents and other people. Consequently, the child will begin to say "my daddy" or "my mommy". The child will begin to tell the difference between his/her toys, his/her clothes and other children's belongings, and parents.

The ego must evolve in order for the child to become independent and manifest his self-determinism. This differentiation helps a lot in this process of evolution of the ego.

The differentiation itself is a stage of evolution. Once the child's mind creates the habit of differentiation, two forms of senses emerge:

- A sense of possessiveness
- A sense of ownership

The child will begin to say, "It's mine", which means, "I own it".

Once the child begins to see differences, he/she has lost his innocence as I have defined it above.

The perception of oneness is no more. He/she will begin to not want people to touch his/her belongings, and not want to share his/her food, toys, and parents with others. The ego has now evolved from the state of possessiveness and ownership into a state of <u>protectiveness</u>.

When the ego feels like it possesses something, it creates the belief that it owns the thing. In relationship for example, lovers feel like they own each other. This feeling usually emerges from the beginning of the relationship. When the ego feels like it owns something, it seeks to protect it. This desire to protect is called <u>attachment</u>.

Once the ego is locked into attachment, it becomes the <u>selfish ego</u>.

However, do not run too quick in labeling this "selfishness" as bad. I am not done.

There are two kinds of selfishness. For example, in case of an emergency in an airplane, you must first take care of your own safety, before thinking about helping someone else. This is also a safety requirement. It is selfish. But it is positive.

This selfishness is based on the simple common sense that you must first be safe before you can lend a hand to another person. Therefore, this selfishness, which is attached to our survival, is not something bad. If you cannot provide for yourself, you cannot provide for others. It is simply common sense.

However, there is of course another kind of selfishness. The one you are authorized to label as negative, if you wish. As the ego remains for too long in the state of protectiveness, this second form of selfishness occurs through false perception. <u>"I have to take care of myself</u>

by keeping what belongs to me safe". As we said it before, when the ego feels like it owns something, it seeks to protect it.

From this desire to protect, the ego becomes victim of the belief that unless it protects what it owns, it may lose it or someone may destroy it. This is where everything changes.

This belief increases and creates an illusion that there is not enough of what the ego possesses. This illusion is caused by the belief in lack and scarcity.

This belief in lack and scarcity hunts the ego with the false impression that if the ego gives or shares what it has with others, it will finish, and the ego will suffer. Out of this false impression, the second selfishness is born, the negative one, the sinful nature or the carnal mind.

The journey of the ego is not yet over. This second selfishness also grows into a higher illusion, where the ego starts believing that, not only it must not give or share, it must also keep on accumulating more of what it already has.

Unfaithfulness, or lust for example, is the manifestation of this egoistic spirit of accumulation. Accumulation to its extreme degree turns into greed.

This desire to accumulate negates the spirit of contentment and gratitude.

The bible says that the unfaithful are trapped by evil desires (Proverbs 11: 6).

In this state of continual accumulation, the individual is "cursed" with non-satisfaction. He has cursed himself with his own belief. He wants more and more of what it already has.

Now, you can say that the individual has arrived at the pinnacle of selfishness. The individual will accumulate, hoard, and become greedy, careless, and fearful. It can even come to kill, lie, and hurt to accumulate more and more. No matter how much he/she has, he/she will still believe that it is not enough.

Now, before I proceed on teaching you about the ego, it is important for me to explain to you two important things: Who you really are and what the Soul is. Unless I explain these two elements to you, you will still be seriously confused in your understanding of the ego.

However, before we proceed, try to re-read or revise the part 1 and part 2 to make sure you fully understood the ego.

What have you learned so far?

_____
_____
_____
_____
_____
_____
_____
_____
_____
_____
_____
_____
_____
_____
_____
_____

Part 3

Who are you?

I spoke to you about the basic ego, which is "I". Now, I will talk to you about "I am". When you say, "I am", you are simply aware of your existence, nothing more and nothing less.

However, when you say, *"I am a man"*, you become a consciousness. There is a difference between *"I am"* and *"I am something"*. Here is the difference you must not forget.

"I am" is *pure awareness.*

"I am something" *is consciousness*.

Awareness is not consciousness.

Consciousness is "I am" identifying itself with something or a thought.

No thought, no consciousness.

No thought, no mind, no consciousness.

Awareness becomes consciousness only when it identifies itself with something else. Did you get this very well? Please, read it again.

When you say, *"I am"*, you are in pure awareness, or a state of *"no mind"* or in the NOW. Identification could take you out of the present moment, drop you in the past, or fire you into the future like a skyrocket.

Now, when you say for example *"I am Christ"*, you become a Christ-consciousness, which is nothing else but pure consciousness.

When you say, *"I am a man"*, you become man-consciousness. You may have a female body, but when the consciousness moving in the body *is man-consciousness*, you will act like a man. It goes the same way with men acting like women.

So who are you? You are pure awareness with no fixed identity. When you say, *"I am that I am"*, you are awakening your true state of beingness, which is pure awareness.

"I am that I am", this is the state of the true peace that surpasses all understandings. This is the state of enlightenment, God-realization or love-realization. This is the state of salvation on earth. You have entered into the inner kingdom in the here and now, in this present moment.

I was counseling a lady one time and while she was complaining about her husband, I asked her repeatedly: "What is your husband doing to you now, at this moment?"

She argued with the question, but then waited for a moment and answered, "right now, he is not doing anything to me."

Then I said, "It is true that in the present moment, in the kingdom of God within you and me, your husband is faultless. But if you are willing to see him in the past by stepping out of this moment, you will find him guilty, you cannot forgive him, and you will seek to punish him.

Yet, all the answers God will give you to deal with the situation, all the powers he will channel to you, and all the strength you will need, are in this present moment." Within this state of *"I am that I am"*, you do not seek to become anything. You are already everything. This everything is God, Christ, or the essence of goodness that lies at the core of all living things and the universe itself.

The expression *"I am Christ"* is something that should come by inspiration, not by will. The Christ does not need to prove anything to itself. It does not need to remind itself of what it is. I call it "it", because the Christ is both male and female. It is the essence of God. We learn in **Hebrews 1: 13**, "The Son is the radiance of God's glory and the exact representation of his being,"

The Christ is the son or the seed of God. It is the image and the likeness of God. It is YOU. It comes on its own into pure awareness, just like you would naturally feel hungry and say *"I am hungry"*. You are compelled by a divine force within to say the thought *"I am the Christ of God"*.

What have you learned so far?

_____

_____

_____

_____

_____

_____

_____

_____

_____

_____

_____

_____

_____

_____

_____

_____

_____

_____

_____

_____

_____

Part 4

What is the Soul?

The Soul is made of LIFE-SUBSTANCE and THOUGHTS. The Soul is basically an energetic field of information. Thoughts are information. Within this field there are preloaded data, which are in charge of making our bodily organs work. The Soul is also impregnated with a mechanism called the subconscious mind.

Now, let me make something clear. There is a subconscious mind as mechanism, and there is a subconscious mind as a department of the Soul. Many people are confused with these two a lot.

The subconscious mind as mechanism functions like an automatic principle of cause and effect. And there is a subconscious mind that operates as a storage house where all experiences are kept as memories and thoughts.

Now, let us continue. The creator has preloaded some information in the Soul, which the mechanism as subconscious mind uses to make the body function. The data given to this mechanism constitute the *cause*. The result it generates as bodily functions is the *effect*.

Now, the Soul has another department called the subconscious mind, which is almost like a computer hard drive. It keeps records of everything we think, feel, say, do and experience on earth. It is also referred to as *the book of life* where our name (nature/character) is written or imprinted.

Below this department of the Soul (subconscious mind), there is another mind, called the superconscious mind. This superconscious mind is the same as pure awareness. It is the kingdom of God within. It is the home of *"I am"*.

This superconscious mind is a realm of perfect ideas, beauty, happiness, love and all the divine gifts you could think of. If you have ever experienced something like a hunch or an intuition, and you followed it and had a positive result, know that it came from the superconscious mind. It is your inner guide.

"The heart is deceitful above all things and beyond cure. Who can understand it" **(Jeremiah 17: 9)?** The subconscious mind is the heart of man, it is deceitful, because it contains all recorded data from experiences good as well as bad.

The superconscious mind is your true heart, the heart of God in you, the Home of the Christ and the Holy Spirit. The bible mentioned this heart saying, "The purposes of a person's heart are deep waters, but one who has insight draws them out" **(Proverbs 20: 5).** It takes divine wisdom to hear from God within.

The subconscious mind or the Soul's hard drive is between the superconscious mind and another department of the Soul called the conscious mind. When you are eating and you know that you are eating, you are then using the conscious mind. We use the conscious mind to analyze, to connect with our experiences, to research, and to connect to the outside world.

So what is the Soul? It is the combination of the conscious mind, the subconscious mind, and the superconscious mind. The

Soul is made of these three layers. The Soul itself could be seen as a big Mind with three different functions, or one tree with three branches.

Now, how does the ego interact within the Soul? This is very important to know. This is where you will learn how to live with yourself and others.

What have you learned so far?

_____

_____

_____

_____

_____

_____

_____

_____

_____

_____

_____

_____

_____

_____

_____

Part 5

The ego and the Soul

When the basic ego evolves into its tree dimensions of:

- *Possessiveness*
- *Ownership*
- *Protectiveness*

It forms a <u>three-layer-pattern</u> within the conscious mind. We use these threefold layer to see the world, and to interpret reality for our own survival.

You can easily identify this threefold-layer-pattern when you interact with the world around you in everything you say or do. Just pay attention to it when you say, *"I am hungry". "I am going to work".*

When you say, *"my boss", "my bank account", "my car", "my family", "this house is mine", "I am late", "I am tired", "it's me", "my husband",* and so forth, you are using the basic ego in its threefold pattern for your survival.

Now, everything you absorb from the outside world as good or bad through this threefold-layer-pattern of the basic ego, form beliefs in your subconscious mind.

Now, these beliefs act like independent personalities through the mechanism of the subconscious mind. It acts like the law of cause and effect.

Jesus said, "A good man brings good things out of the good stored up in him, and an evil man brings evil things out of the evil stored up in him" (**Matthew 12: 35**).

The data you put into the Soul as a cause produces an effect. This effect is called a *"reaction"*, because you are not willingly expressing them. They come out on their own. This is also the case of addictions. You don't choose to be angry, but you will be angry anyways. You are living like a program.

At the conscious level, you may not want to smoke, but you will smoke. You may not want to lust, but you will lust. You may not want to eat, but you will eat. You may not want to be angry, but you will be angry. You may not want to insult, but you will find yourself insulting. Why?

Let me explain it to you. Everything you absorb from the outside world and that enters into your Soul splits itself into two categories. The bad data are separate from the good data.

All pains and sufferings are in a separate "folder". The beliefs in scarcity, lack, accumulation, and stinginess are in the same "folder" as well as all your past painful experiences. The beliefs in abundance, giving, and sharing are in a different "folder" as all your past happy experiences.

Now, pay attention to this. When you are in the state of pure awareness, which is *"I am"*, the mechanism called subconscious mind activates wonderful ideas and feelings from the superconscious mind and causes you to act from the impulse of love. We call this inspiration or the Spirit moving through you.

However, when you are in the state of consciousness, which is *"I am this and that"*, one of the folders (good or bad) in the subconscious mind (storage) is activated in the Soul and you act either good or bad. This is why many people recommend positive thinking. It is simply a way for them to tell you that you should always be activating the good folder.

The negative folder is the selfish ego, which is victim of accumulation and many illusions, thus seeks to hoard and hurt others.

The positive folder is the moral ego, which feels and acts good. It does so, not out of inspiration but out of ethical principles or moral values found in the society and books.

Positive thoughts are different from divine thoughts. Positive thoughts are programs from good experiences stored up in the Soul. They could be stimulated.

Divine thoughts are not uploaded from experiences. You are created with them. They abide in superconscious mind. You are superconscious mind. Awareness and superconscious mind are ONE.

We activate the superconscious mind by being present, by being here and NOW, by interpreting nothing, and by labeling nothing.

Only the positive folder and the negative folder could be activated by a stimulus from outside or from new experiences.

Unfortunately, we are not usually in control of the kind of folder we will activate. We are constantly stimulated by the realities around us.

These reactions from the subconscious happen spontaneously. We don't often have time to analyses them. Before you think, the negative words are already spoken, and the negative decision is already taken.

They happen almost unnoticed. We fall into them, because we are not aware most of the times.

"An angry person stirs up conflict, and a hot-tempered person commits many sins" **(Proverbs 29: 22).**

Every negative feeling or emotion makes you unconscious. And anytime you are unconscious, you put yourself in reactive mode. You no longer have control of your thoughts, words, or actions. Anything could come out of you.

In **Luke 6: 43** we read, "No good tree bears bad fruit, nor does a bad tree bear good fruit. Be aware that our environment acts like an independent stimulus. What we see, we hear, we touch, we say, we smell or we do, could easily stimulate the negative folder, before we even notice.

However, there are solutions, and they are spiritual in nature, that one could use to control the outside stimuli.

So what is the ego that most people struggle against, and how does it function in the Soul? This ego, which is not the basic one for our survival, is simply a folder that contains a bundle of selfish beliefs and negative data within your soul that has been absorbed from experiences.

We can categorize the grip of this negative ego unto what I like to call *seven nails.* These are the nails the ego uses to torment and enslave the human Soul. Every struggle you go through can be overcome by conducting critical self-analyses.

What have you learned so far?

_____

_____

_____

_____

_____

_____

_____

_____

_____

_____

_____

_____

_____

_____

_____

_____

_____

_____

_____

_____

Part 6

Critical self-analysis (CSA)

Critical self-analysis is the only and supreme way to return to your Self, the Christ within, to remove the masks, to transcend the veils, to cancel the personalities, and to set your *"I am"* free from the snares of the ego.

Setting the "I am" free from negative personalities is salvation. When these personalities are crucified, your true Self is resurrected into a new life.

As Christians, we see the death of Jesus on the cross as the death of the ego (accumulation of negative personalities). As we believe that it is our ego that died with him, we absorb that belief into our consciousness through faith, and declare that we, as the ego, no longer live and that we are a new creation.

Paul advised us, "Do not lie to each other, since you have taken off your old self with its practices, and have put on the new self, which is being renewed in knowledge in the image of its Creator" (**Colossians 3: 9-10**)

All other spiritual and therapeutic means such as Soul Treatment, counseling, and deliverance come into play, simply because most people are not able to conduct a proper critical self-analysis, and keep consistency in doing it using the word of God and the power of the Holy Ghost. Self-deliverance is something possible to everyone.

In some dramatic cases, these images or personalities become so strong and energized that they act like "demons" or "evil spirits". I am not saying that this is what demons and evil spirits are all about. Yet, my focus here is not to teach about such things. Tramp spirits do possess Souls when they find a connecting link within these Souls or emptiness.

I want to show you what these seven nails of the ego or carnal mind are, and how you can transcend them through critical self-analysis. CSA is a personal therapy based on faith and the understanding of who you are. It is a surgery you conduct on your own Soul, to improve yourself, your relationships, your affairs, and your Life.

Most people wonder why they are born again through confession, but they still struggle with the same sinful inclinations. The answer is CSA.

For your critical self-analysis to work, you need four tools:

- *Honesty*
- *Integrity*
- *Tolerance*
- *Consistency*

If any one of these four elements is missing, you will not have the result you expect.

Honesty is the truth you tell yourself. When you see something in you that you know is not "good", you must admit it to yourself. Do not lie to yourself. Do not be in denial. Do not see black and call it white. You must love yourself enough to tell yourself the truth.

"Honesty guides good people; dishonesty destroys treacherous people" (**Proverbs 11: 3**).

You must have integrity. *Integrity* here means to only consider what you have seen and discovered about yourself, through reasoning, common sense, and experiences, and what you have judged as real to you.

If you see anger in you, let it be that you are the one who have seen it first and recognized it; and not something that someone else has told you. But rather something that came from your own work of self-examination.

Tolerance means you must not beat yourself up, because of the weakness you are seeing in yourself. You must not carry guilt. Always remember that you are not these weaknesses. Always remember to let the ego be what it is, and allow yourself to be what you are: *"I am"*.

Consistency means discipline and ability to stick to what you believe. If you don't believe in what you are doing, you will not keep on doing it. Give yourself a schedule and stick with the schedule. CSA is a lifetime journey. Therefore, you must not start with the consciousness to arrive somewhere, to reach a certain point, or to meet a final goal. Do it, because you believe in it, and because you want to be a better person. That is it. Therefore fall in love with the act of doing it.

What have you learned?

_____

_____

_____

_____

_____

_____

_____

_____

_____

_____

_____

_____

_____

_____

_____

_____

_____

_____

_____

_____

_____

Part 7

How to conduct the CSA?

"The soul of the sluggard craves and gets nothing, But the soul of the diligent is made fat" (**Proverbs 13: 4**).

If you do your CSA daily or with diligence, you will always improve daily. It is preferable to conduct your CSA every evening before you go to bed. This is a good suggestion. If you make a decision to do this for life, there is no way you will not become happier, clearer, and more peaceful.

The process will take seven steps:

1. *Overviewing*
2. *Browsing*
3. *Scanning*
4. *Seeing*
5. *Identifying*
6. *Sorting out*
7. *Affirming*

Overviewing

You will go over the entire day in your mind. You will start from the moment you awake to the moment you are ready to sleep. This is a suggested way to start: *"I see myself waking up"*; *"I see myself brushing my teeth"* etc. Go slowly and breathe between each three segments of events until you have gone through the last one. Each segment of event is called a track. The whole track is called a film. Do nothing else but just counting the whole day to yourself.

Browsing

The browsing consists of locating some key events that took place in tracks. It is almost as if you were giving a review to a film that had been played by you and others (People you interacted with during the day). To do this properly you must look at the film and allow yourself to be reminded of some interactions and events that kind of stayed with you for some reasons. Write those interactions and events down. These interactions and events I call them "the stockers".

Scanning

As you analyze the stockers, you will simply notice your feelings in order to classify them. You make a table with two columns. The stockers that make you feel good; you write them in one column. The stockers that make you feel bad, you write them down in the other column.

Seeing

Seeing here means the ability to see things for what they are, and let them go without being attached to them. You want to be a witness and nothing else. You want to be an observer, and nothing else. And this, you will do only with the positive stockers or the stockers that made you feel good. You will take them one by one, and see the kind of "ego nail" they correspond to, and let them go. For example, today your boss praised you in front of everyone at work.

You felt good about it. But, you must not be attached to that feeling, or it will begin to control your performance at work, give you the pressure of the fear of making mistakes or disappoint your boss. It will make you lose the freedom of being yourself.

Identifying

This feeling you registered from the experience with your boss is connected to the nail of the ego that says: *"I am more important than everyone"*. You must identify it quickly and remove it.

Sorting out

The sorting out is a reminder. You have to remind yourself that there is nothing wrong with feeling good. The issue is when the ego takes the feeling to enslave you and cause you to lose your freedom. The sorting out is the ability to make a difference between the fact and what the ego uses the fact for. You will be able to conduct the sorting out by reading about its corresponding ego's nail. The sorting out is simply a mental activity to remember. It is important to do it before you move to the affirmation.

Affirming

To affirm is to bring yourself back to the center of your universe. All feelings, good or bad, take you off the center of your universe with the intention to occupy it. The feeling that occupies the center will control the entire universe. Your universe is all about everything your mind is connected to in your life such as your job, your spouse, your children, and your routines.

Let us say you never detached yourself from the "feeling good" from the experience with your boss, and you ended up making a mistake at work, and your boss said, *"I am disappointed in you."* This will generate a "feeling bad" data. You will start blaming yourself.

This will affect your universe, meaning your interaction with yourself, spouse, children, and your routines will start showing a lot of negativities.

But, ask yourself what is really controlling your universe at that point. It is not the negative feeling. It is the *"feeling good"* you attached your Soul to at the first place. Nothing negative comes into the Soul unless there was an opposite data of that feeling first recorded into the Soul.

To every negative feeling, there is a previous recorded opposite feeling, which will be *good feeling*. If the good feeling occupies the center, the bad one will later on be created right at the center out of the good feeling.

Another example

Let us say a friend of yours buys you an ice cream every Friday. He did this for six straight months. Then, one day, while you were sitting with another friend of yours, he came with an ice cream and gave it to the other friend instead.

If you feel angry, jealous, and unhappy, this is not your friend's problem. He is free to give an ice cream to whomever he wants. You cannot take people's freedom away from them.

The only time you do that is when you have lost your own freedom. Losing your own freedom means you left the center of your universe for a moment, and allowed a feeling to take over the center.

During this period of six months, you created an attachment between your Soul and your friend's kindness. You should not have done this. You became addicted to his kindness. You ended up believing that his kindness is your right. So when he does not buy an ice cream for you, you end up insanely believing that he violated your right.

Your anger, jealousy, and unhappiness are created from the *"good feeling"* you have allowed to occupy the center of your universe during these six months.

Your affirmations are to detach you from all *good feelings*. You have to be able to create them and speak them between each inhaling and exhaling for 15 minutes straight. You must do this for all "good feelings" on the list for that day. The truth is, you need nothing added to you in order to be happy. You are happiness itself. Happiness does not come from outside. It comes from within. This must be your mindset.

Sample of affirmation (15 minutes)

*"I now let go of this good feeling that came from … (**name the event**). I am perfectly free, and essentially happy. I need nothing to make me more than what I am."*

Now, if there are only negative feelings, you will create their opposite before you affirm. The opposite is somewhere in the Soul. It had been uploaded there in the past.

I will now give you an example:

Let's say that you are feeling bad because your spouse yelled at you today at the supermarket and your friend saw you. This may be because in the past you praised your husband to the same friend. Now, you are feeling terrible, feeling like a liar, and feeling ashamed wondering about what your friend is thinking about you.

What you have to do is to create the data of the positive message you told your friend. It does not have to be in the exact words. You can write something like, *"My husband is a wonderful and gentle man".*

Now, you may ask yourself if you have this character to praise something or people to others, so that they may see you in a certain way. If you do, then locate the corresponding ego's nail. In this case it will be, *"You have more than everyone".*

Then the suggested affirmation will be: *"I am totally what I am. My husband is totally who he is. I have no need to prove myself to anyone. I am free"*

If it is about your house for instance:

"I am totally what I am. My house is totally what it is. I have no need to prove myself to anyone. I am free."

P.S: It is beneficial to conduct a research on the characters you want to change.

What have you learned so far?

_____

_____

_____

_____

_____

_____

_____

_____

_____

_____

_____

_____

_____

_____

Part 8

The seven nails of the ego

"There are six things the LORD hates, seven that are detestable to him: haughty eyes, a lying tongue, hands that shed innocent blood, a heart that devises wicked schemes, feet that are quick to rush into evil, a false witness who pours out lies and a person who stirs up conflict in the community" (**Proverbs 6: 16-19**).

The seven nails of the ego are the causes of the seven things that are detestable to God. In reality all the seven nails are branches to the sinful mind or the ego. The ego or the enemy is one and it comes to attack you from one way, but flees through seven ways or seven personalities (nails).

The Bible says in **Deuteronomy 28: 7**, *"The LORD will conquer your enemies when they attack you. They will attack you from one direction, but they will scatter from you in seven!"*

The "nails" or the "grips" of the ego are nothing else but beliefs. Beliefs are vows our mind makes to our heart.

Each belief functions like an independent consciousness and a personality with its own will.

The truth of the matter is that most people have these beliefs but they are not aware of them. These beliefs, nails, grips, or voices are in your unconsciousness. They are recorded in the subconscious mind. It is because they are unconscious that they are able to rule the Soul and negatively influence your life.

Some of these beliefs sound so well and so good to the ears, that the Soul is seduced by them. This is called arrogance. It stops people from wanting to change.

Once they seduce the Soul, the Soul begins to act them out with absolute ignorance. These beliefs are the root-cause of the way we think, the way we feel, the way we speak and the way we act.

These beliefs or nails are the very substance of man's inability and incapacity to experience happiness and bliss to the fullest.

Being aware of these nails is the first step to be free from them. This awareness is not just about knowing the beliefs, but fully understanding what they do and how they could be recognized.

What have you learned?

_____

_____

_____

_____

_____

_____

_____

_____

_____

_____

_____

_____

_____

_____

_____

First Nail

"You are the body"

This is the nail of the ego that creates within the Soul the personality that is materialist.

"To the person who pleases him, God gives wisdom, knowledge and happiness, but to the sinner he gives the task of gathering and storing up wealth to hand it over to the one who pleases God. This too is meaningless, a chasing after the wind" (**Ecclesiastes 2: 26**).

The materialist, even if he/she wants to, cannot give any importance to his/her own Soul evolution or personal spiritual growth. Jesus called our personal spiritual growth *"seeking first the kingdom of God"*.

The true meaning of being a materialist is forgetting that happiness is not material or physical but abstract and spiritual.

If you believe that you are the body, you will evidently be concerned only with what you will eat, what you will wear, what you will drink, and where you will sleep.

Jesus said to his disciples: *"Therefore I tell you, do not worry about your life, what you will eat; or about your body, what you will wear. For life is more than food, and the body more than clothes. Consider the ravens: They do not sow or reap, they have no storeroom or barn; yet God feeds them. And how much more valuable you are than birds!"* (**Luke 12: 22-13**)

As a materialist, your entire life revolves around what you can see, touch, hear, taste, and feel.

The materialist believes in a higher power only when he is in trouble and might lose some of his possessions. Even this belief is not real.

He does not seek to understand spiritual ideas, God, the universe, because he is not so much concerned with spiritual values.

"Wisdom and money can get you almost anything, but only wisdom can save your life" (**Ecclesiastes 7: 12**).

I-am-the-body-consciousness" believes only in material things. Consequently, he cannot see himself more than the body. He perceives God the same way he perceives himself.

It is because of this first nail of, *"I am the body"*, that you are unable to see God as a Spirit, and rather see him as this giant human being with a long white beard sitting on a throne beyond the sky.

It is the same nail of the ego that makes your perception cloudy. Because of this nail, you cannot see beyond your five senses, and your judgment of reality is very limited and carnal.

"For to be carnally minded is death; but to be spiritually minded is life and peace" **(Romans 8: 6).**

As a materialist, when you are faced with difficulties or problems, which are from the realm of the abstract, not physical realities, you find yourself incapable of dealing with them. Instead, fear grabs your mind, heart, and drives you very, very, crazy.

The person whose consciousness is locked in "I am the body" experiences strong mental oppression and depression as a result of anxious thoughts.

Not only can he not solve problems from their abstract nature, (which is finding real solution), he will seek for material means such as money or social intimidation to solve life issues, which cannot really solved that way.

The materialistic personality may use money to try to solve problems, because to him only what is physical brings real answer to problems.

If a person possessed by the materialistic personality is not rich, he or she will use his body-appearance to solve life-issues. This is how people end up in prostitution and gangs. He or she will also find ways to espouse or be with someone who has money, simply to suck life out of that person. Materialists are parasites.

The *"I am the body"* consciousness is also the source of illnesses in the body. Since this consciousness sees the world from the body point of view by measuring his life with his possessions, when he lacks material things, he is angry, unhappy, resentful, and very weary. These negative energies poison the body to make the body's immune system very weak.

Jesus said, *"Watch out! Be on your guard against all kinds of greed; life does not consist in an abundance of possessions"* (**Luke 12: 15**).

Money is the *"god"* that rules the awareness that is locked into the *"I am the body"* consciousness. Why? The reason is not the money itself, but what money can do in the material world. It helps the materialist own more possessions.

The materialist does not understand happiness since it is an abstract concept. Consequently, his superficial joy and happiness are created by money.

This is the reason he sees money as his god. Though he does not call it this way, he may even deny it, but his action clearly portrays someone who has made money their god.

The proof is when money increases, the materialistic personality is happy. When money decreases, he is miserable.

Money tells him how he should feel. He is afraid of the future when money starts decreasing. This is because money is in control of the world of materialists.

People, who are considered as *neat freaks,* are also locked in the same consciousness of *"I am the body"*. Those same people have a hard time considering people's opinions about life, because to them what they think must always be right.

"I am the body" is a personality that could also be very addicted to clothes and everything that will make the person look good in appearance. He is addicted to pleasing people, and cannot wear the same clothes twice. The personality will make him believe that people are paying close attention to what he/she wears. Therefore, he/she is prone to excessive shopping.

What have you learned so far?

_____

_____

_____

_____

_____

_____

_____

_____

_____

_____

_____

_____

_____

_____

_____

_____

_____

_____

_____

_____

_____

Second Nail

*"You are more important
than everyone"*

Though the first nail of the ego, *"you are
the body"* is one of the most powerful
beliefs from the ego, the second nail is
equally dangerous.

All the other six nails have as foundation
the first one. The first nail is the ground
upon which all the other nails stand to
flourish.

It is written that Jesus came to *"free those
who all their lives were held in slavery by
their fear of death"* (**Hebrews 2: 15**).

It is the belief that one is the body that is
the root cause of many fears such as: *the
fear of death, the fear of judgment, the fear
of rejection and so on.*

Happiness and freedom belong to the
realm of the abstract. With a strong belief
that one is the body, the Soul struggles to
shift from illusion into Reality.

Humility is the ability to see everyone as yourself. Yet, many souls love to see differences. This is the true meaning of pride. *"When pride comes, then comes disgrace, but with humility comes wisdom"* (**Proverbs 11: 2**).

"Now if we died with Christ, we believe that we will also live with him" (**Romans 6: 8**).

Pride is spiritual blindness. Blindness is misperception. And the contemplation of death is the greatest pathway to cure pride. Only the contemplation of death could totally remove pride from the Soul. The concept of we are ONE does not sink into the Soul, until the mind sees death.

At death, we are the same. There is no poor. There is no rich. It is this realization that awakes many souls on earth when death strikes. Yet, once they return home from the funeral, the mind once more sinks back into the illusion that we are different. Death is the greatest teacher of life, yet we are stubborn students.

King Salomon, after throwing a serious investigational perception upon his wealth and achievement, concluded, "All these achievement and possessions are ultimately profitless" (**Ecclesiastes 2: 11**).

Souls that love to see themselves above others are usually the most fearful ones. They are afraid to lose their images, their appearance, their status, their position, and so forth.

These souls cannot accept death and sometimes find themselves stuck between the earthly realm and the spiritual realm once they depart from here.

The fear of death and the pain the soul feels when death comes are the results of a strong attachment to the body, which in itself has as a root-belief that one is the body. Please keep in mind that what we are calling body here is beyond what you see in the mirror.

The body encompasses everything that you create an attachment to through your five senses. We are talking about a sensual or a carnal ego, an ego that gives importance to things that have no eternal value. Jesus will ask, *"What good is it for someone to gain the whole world, yet forfeit their soul?"* (**Mark 8: 36**)

The second nail of the ego, which plunges the mind into a delusional belief that one is more important than everyone is, manifests itself usually in a very unusual way. You cannot say "no" to this ego. It will take it personal. You see this ego most of the times in the business world.

For example, when this ego presents a product or services to a client, and the client says, *"No, I am not interested",* this ego will take it personal. It will react with anger and negative emotions towards the client. It will even curse the client under its breath.

This is because it believes that it is more important than the client. It denies the client of his right and freedom to speak his or her mind. This belief comes from the fact that this ego sees the product as itself. When you reject the product, it feels rejected. This is insanity. It also stems from attachment to material things or physical reality.

This is not the end of the insanity. It does not stop there. The next time this ego will have another product, a different kind to sell, once the thought of showing it to the same client will cross its mind, it will make a decision not to. This ego is also resentful.

This ego is in pain for no reason. You notice this second degree of insanity in the fact that both products are different, and the client never did anything wrong. The client simply said *no*. It is possible that the client likes this second product. However, the ego will stop you from going to this client with the product.

Now, the question is, why will you get angry with someone simply because he/she expresses his/her freedom? It does not make any sense. This is what we call arrogance. This ego is also arrogant.

The ego believes it has the right and freedom to show his products to others, yet does not believe that people have the right to say *no*.

This insane inclination to be offended because people express their freedom comes from the unconscious belief that one is more important than others. The truth is we are all the same, and we are all important, because we equally matter as humans.

Remember that this ego likes to be at the center of the world. He wants to control people. Therefore, he has to make himself important in the eyes of others.

I will give you another example. A friend of yours is having a party. This friend did not invite you to the party. This same ego will take this personal and react to it.

Relationships are to be based on freedom in order to grow in true love. This kind of freedom I am talking about here scares the ego a lot. This ego cannot let people be who they want to be, because it needs them in order to grow its wings and fly above them all. At the same time if it does not feel needed, it reacts. This is another form of insanity.

Now, let us think of the sane way to live. Imagine that you see your friend the next day, and still love him the same way, with absolute sincerity, because you remove this second nail of the ego out of your Soul. If your friend has an ego, his/her ego will not be at peace. Your friend will be offended for the fact that you are not reacting to the fact that he/she did not invite you to the party.

If your friend's decision was not based on ego, you will both just move on with the relationship with not restriction.

Sanity gives pure love, because it lives freely and allows people to live freely. You will not be free until you let people experience their own freedom to the fullest. When you embrace freedom within yourself, you will kill this ego.

Expectations are chains we put around people to enslave them. There cannot be true love when the heart is in chains. Those who feel more important than others cannot love.

The insanity of this ego does not stop here. Another example: When you invite someone to a dinner, and the person cannot make it, this ego will also take that personal.

This ego will begin to tell you all kind of stories about your friend, because it likes people to do everything according to its agenda, and it even wants people to change their agenda to suit its own. This is what we call selfishness.

The ego *of "I am more important than everyone,"* also likes to tell others how they should eat, dress, walk, and almost do everything. This is top-class insanity. Some people, who are infected with this ego to the highest degree, remain single for the rest of their lives, simply because this ego keeps on finding something wrong with others.

The amazing thing is this ego will not want anyone to tell it what to do or even make suggestions to it. It sees even suggestions as offenses and makes untrue assumptions out of them.

Consequently, this ego will not seek advices because to this ego, by seeking advices, it is exposing its weaknesses. When this ego lives in you, your life does not improve.

This ego will even prefer to die in suffering, rather than being open about his wounds and find healing. Can you believe this? Yes, it happens. People prefer to die in their misery instead of asking for help.

This ego will even lie to your mind telling you that everyone has their own problems, not to bother them with yours trying to find solutions. It is a lie to keep you under its grip until it finishes you.

When this ego possesses your mind, your life, and heart feel very unfulfilled and unhappy.

You always go under the impression that people are out there to cause you trouble. You are always on your guard and afraid to make friends. You are not even comfortable about the idea of being truly loved.

This particular ego also does something else that is very strange; it will make friends with other egos that behave like it, and will be very, very comfortable to tell its friends everything about itself. Why? Because when egos are together, they are always blind to their own downfall.

However, this ego will stay away from people who can see through its disguises because their love is genuine. True love, even at 15 percent of expression, could make this ego very uncomfortable.

This ego with the nail of *"I am more important"* is very ignorant, but will not seek knowledge. This ego is always hypnotized by the arrogant delusional belief that he already knows. Yet, deep within, it knows it does not know. It has to fool itself to feel "on top" of the world.

This ego possesses people who grew up in some form of *"we've-got-it-all-figured-out"*-type of environment. They have not learned how to deal with life's issues and be vulnerable. They face major trials alone, some of which could have been less intense had they been vulnerable.

The environment they were brought up in was presided by a controlling system that leaves no room for people to be free and to do what they want to do.

Their lives are usually planned and programmed unconsciously, and they grow up with much insecurity. They have to satisfy the program the environment created within them. They are not free.

This ego is at the root of uncontrolled reactions such as frustrations, rage, anger, and the *"my-way or- the-highway"* character.

Those, whose souls are under the strong grip of this kind of ego, suffer unusual and strange neck pain from time to time.

They can also experience sudden heart palpitations. They sometimes suffer from some strange eye aches that come and go, causing headaches and pain behind the ears area. This is because every ego releases its energy or vibration into the body cells.

What have you learned so far?

_____

_____

_____

_____

_____

_____

_____

_____

_____

_____

_____

_____

_____

_____

_____

_____

_____

_____

_____

_____

_____

_____

Third Nail

"You have more than everyone"
This is the ego that loves to always be prioritized. It likes to be acknowledged and recognized for works it did. If it does not get this sort of attention, it is not happy at all.

Your true essence is Love, and "Love is not self-seeking" (**1 Corinthians 13: 5**).

This ego is addicted to reputation and prizes, trophies, certificates and the likes. When it possesses the mind, one could become addicted to his career and neglect important things of life; things that make us experience ourselves as bliss and love.

In everything, this ego wants attention. It wants the whole attention for itself. It suffers from jealousy and envy, and likes to see anyone who seems to do well fail. This ego has a tendency of becoming a sadist.

People's failure gives this ego a hidden feeling of pleasure; for to him other people's failure means an occasion for it to be above everyone else. This ego is curse by its own false belief that success is a finite idea, that when much people get it, there will be none left. It is insane.

This ego compares itself a lot with others. When it hears that someone has received a promotion, or bought a new house, or bought a new car, or won the lottery, it is unhappy, yet will fake to be happy around this person.

This ego beats you down. It makes you miserable by comparing other people's success to your failures, to keep you in a resentful state of consciousness, thus making you blind to see your uniqueness and your own potentials.

This ego is also very intellectual, and it loves to impress others with its social status. It only respects people who are intellectual, and it looks down on others who are more simple and creative, unless they have money.

This ego works hard to accumulate a lot of money so that others may see it on top of the world, and come to ask him for favor. In reality, it is not a way to serve that this ego is looking for, but instead it is looking for ways to be worshiped.

When this ego is not asked a favor, yet knows that someone else is consulted for help instead of it, it takes this very personal and asks: *"how is it that you did not come to me?"* This is because it believes that someone was given more importance than it.

The problem is this ego likes to use its possessions or whatever it believes it has more of, to control others. This ego likes to control a lot.

This ego is also victim of a very strange form of hallucination. For example, in a group, it feels like it has to be given more tasks than everyone else. If he does not see this, it starts to make a false belief that it is not appreciated or valued, and becomes very frustrated. This is because this ego likes recognition and applauses.

This ego also likes public drama, as long as it does not negatively affect it. When someone is in trouble, it will start speaking loud in public so people could hear what happens. It will raise its voice trying to sound wise, and laugh hard to draw attention concerning someone else's problem. It uses someone else's issue to make itself look important.

Your true essence is Love, and "Love does not delight in evil, but rejoices with Truth" **(1 Corinthians 13: 6).**

This form of ego is very competitive, because it wants to always have more than others. It will do anything to make its rivals appear weak through gossips and hurtful criticism.

This ego is very cynical, yet always makes sure no one blemishes its own reputation. When this ego comes to lose what it has, it will start blaming others, even God. It never sees its own shortcomings, because it has to feel more important in order to feel that it has more than everyone does.

The most powerful foolish thing about this ego is that it believes that without its presence, people around it cannot make it. This is not because it seeks to inspire them, but because it sees others weak and incapable. Because of this lie, it always seeks to know people's business and intrude in matters that do not concern it.

People who suffer from this ego often time have the habit of chewing their nails uncontrollably, or chewing on random small objects; they can do this even in public. In addition, they always have to hold something in their hands to play with while talking.

These are signs of insecurity. These people often stutter due to suppressed anger for not being recognized for achievements, or works they believe they should be honored for. They might also experience abnormal hair loss when the influence of this ego on the Soul intensifies.

What have you learned so far?

_____

_____

_____

_____

_____

_____

_____

_____

_____

_____

_____

_____

_____

_____

_____

_____

_____

_____

_____

_____

_____

Fourth Nail

"You are wiser than everyone"

If you believe that you are wiser than others, then you are not wise, because wisdom cannot be measured. It is an inspiration.

You are Love, your true essence is Love, and "if you have the gift of prophecy and can fathom all mysteries and all knowledge, and if you have a faith that can move mountains, but do not have love, you are nothing" (**1 Corinthians 13: 2**).

Wisdom is inspiration. You cannot measure inspiration. How can you measure infinity?

Wisdom is something to connect to. Some are just more connected to it than others. Yet, wisdom itself cannot be quantified. The wise knows this.

You cannot measure or quantify the unlimited. This nail of the ego makes communication with others very hard.

People who suffer from this nail believe that everyone else is stupid, and only they are smart enough to know what is right.

Wisdom and knowledge are not the same. There are also two kinds of wisdom.

What we call understanding gives birth to knowledge, and knowledge gives wisdom. Yet, this wisdom born of knowledge is not ultimate wisdom.

This wisdom is a simple classification of data (knowledge).

This classification allows one to make practical use of data learned in order to facilitate communication and provoke action.

Anyone can acquire this type of wisdom through knowledge thus *sound* wise.

You do not want to *sound* wise. You want to be wise. You want to speak from inspiration, from the infinite source of knowingness. The wisdom born out of accumulation of data, or born out of knowledge depends on knowledge for the rest of its life. It has its own lifespan.

If knowledge is wrong, this wisdom is also wrong. In fact, sages do not consider this wisdom born out of accumulated data as wisdom, but as a practical knowledge.

True wisdom is inspirational. True wisdom is a world of understanding that opens up from within. It is improvised, meaning spontaneous. This true wisdom cannot be attained by a consciousness that is under the influence of this nail of "*I am wiser than everyone*".

I will give you an illustration to help you understand the difference between the first wisdom and the second wisdom.

Two men were walking by a lake in Jerusalem 2000 years ago. Suddenly a roman soldier approached them demanding they pay their taxes. One of them reached in his pocket, took out some money and paid the roman soldier.

The other man stepped into the lake, caught a fish, and took the money out of the mouth of the fish to pay his tax.

The first man had the money on him. The second man did not have the money on him. The second man, compelled by Spirit and moved by inspiration, brought the money into existence.

This is the difference between these two types of wisdom. True wisdom, you never have it. It comes on its own. It works with a greater power, or I should say a great mind. It works with faith. It works with creative energy.

True wisdom cannot be accumulated, nor stored up in the mind.

True wisdom is not memorized. It comes to you when you need it. This is called inspiration. It is like a daily bread. You eat it just for the day. When tomorrow comes, new bread will come.

The sage would tell you, *"All I know is that I know nothing"*. This is true wisdom.

To *have* knowledge is temporary. To *become* knowledge is eternal. What you have you can lose. What you are you cannot lose.

This nail of the ego, *"you are wiser than everyone"*, is to stop you from becoming knowledge or connecting to the mind of the omniscient in you. I call it God.

To become knowledge is to know true wisdom. To have knowledge could make you arrogant. Those who are under the influence of this nail are not teachable. They find faults in everything people say. Yet, the wise man learns from everyone. The wise man does not despise correction and improvement, because he knows that inspiration flows through unpredicted vessels.

People infected with this ego also have hard time seeing the good side of things. They want their opinions to prevail at all times. This is an intellectual arrogance.

This nail works together with the second nail of *"you are more important than everyone"*. Those who suffer from this fourth nail often suffer from the second nail as well. It is a pattern.

They do not ask for advice. They are ashamed to seek for help. Moreover, they cannot stand the idea that someone may know more than they do. They resist people who are connected to inspiration. They usually make negative comments and criticism about those who operate are from true wisdom.

The way to true wisdom is humility. This humility starts from the awareness that there is an inexhaustible fountain of wisdom within all humans, and we all simply need to tap into it. This wisdom belongs to no one, for it comes from God alone.

I will explain this to you with an illustration. Two women from a remote place in Africa went to the river to draw some water.

After going back and forth many times, trying to fill up their jars at home, one of them started to give an evil eye to the other.

The one the evil eye is been given to asked, *"My sister, why are you looking at me this way? Have I done something wrong?"*

The other woman replied, *"Why are you taking more water than I? Your basin is too big. You are taking too much water from the river".* This is insane. She did not create the water or the river, but she believes she has the right to control how much can be drawn.

This is the exact insanity this nail of the ego is all about. The river is the unlimited fountain of wisdom within the Soul. It is for no one.

The minute you want to take more than everyone, you become insane. It's not something to keep for oneself. It is there for everyone. It is unlimited.

What have you learned so far?

_____

_____

_____

_____

_____

_____

_____

_____

_____

_____

_____

_____

_____

_____

_____

_____

_____

_____

_____

_____

_____

Fifth Nail

"You need to be right"

First, let's talk about the idea of "need". In reality, we do not really *need* anything. We do not. The idea of *need* suggests an acknowledgement of lack and limitations.

How could creative beings see lack and limitations? Lack and limitations are ideas in mind, which the mind projects into the outside world. Should we need anything at all, it will be nothing else but our own selves.

All that you really need is you. Think about it. Nothing is truly lacking. Okay, let me explain myself.

Let us say you believe you need a car. The question should be: Where is the car? Of course, at the dealer's shop.

Is the car lacking or missing? No. The car already exists. The only thing is, it exists somewhere else, but it is not lacking.

The idea of lack refers to an absence of that which one believes he needs.

What you need in order to get the car to your driveway is nothing else but you. *You need* to take the necessary steps to get the car from wherever it may be located, into your driveway.

What we need is ourselves. There are no other real needs out there.

When you falsely believe that something is truly lacking or missing, you are, with no doubt, also accepting the fact that there are limitations, which are not truly there, but in your mind.

You see space and time as limitations, because only space and time stand between you and the car dealer's shop.

You believe you will need time to get the car. You believe you are separate from it. In truth, there are no limitations. You are simply hallucinating. Space and time are in your awareness.

When you are passionate about someone, you see no time and time moving fast. This is to tell you that what you even call time is your own mind measuring your movements through a process.

If you are doing something boring, time runs slow and becomes heavier. So where is time? Your mind is the time. It is the mind that uses itself to fabricate time as limitations.

In **Psalm 23: 1**, David spoke a powerful truth, "The Lord is my shepherd, I shall not want", which really means practically speaking, "The Spirit of God within me is the guidance to my perception, I cannot see a need or something lacking."

You are not separate from anything either. If I remove all the buildings and people out of the way, you and the car will be in the same space. You know this to be true. You know it. Even your imagination is incapable of lying to you about this. We do not have a need. We are simply unconscious of ourselves.

When we become conscious of ourselves, and begin to see that we could get and receive anything we want, all limitations will be uprooted from the mind and the veil of all hallucinations ripped apart. Then we will come to melt into time and space. We become one with them. We see no separation. We receive what we want by moving ourselves to it, and attracting it to us.

It is a lie of the ego to make you believe that something is missing; something is lacking. This will consequently take away your peace. This nail of the ego moves your awareness completely outside, and keeps you unconscious most of the time. You will see yourself more anxious than at peace, and you cannot hold faith in heart for too long.

When the illusion of needs attacks the desire to be right, one becomes very prideful and cannot listen to others. The ego unceasingly will repeat, *"I need to be right, I have to be right, I want to be right, I must be right"*, so on and so forth.

Pride is born out of the belief in needs. Wanting to be right is wanting to prove another wrong. In reality, no one is right and no one is wrong. Everyone is living in his/her own reality.

I will give you an example; snakes for instance are dangerous symbols in the western culture. They are even seen as evil. However, they are worshipped in some eastern cultures as symbol of wisdom. Who is right? Who is wrong?

All killings and irrational actions in the world come from the belief that one needs something. Out of this belief rises one's own interpretation of reality. We create fragmented realities out of which needs appear real. These fragmented realities are just separate thoughts created by the ego.

We do not need to be right, but to know the truth at the center of our own being.

There is no truth in trying to prove another person's wrong, defining reality from your own world, interpreting events, or trying to impose things on others. This is why Jesus was silent when he was asked to defend himself about the lies spoken against him.

All one needs, is to know the truth at the center of his own being, and voice it out plainly when it is really needed, with no impulse to prove someone wrong.

Simply watch your ego act up when someone speaks a lie or gossip about you. You will be amazed of what you will be hearing in your mind. Just try this for yourself.

The need to want to be right is false judgment based on appearance, or self-righteousness. Jesus said, "Do not judge according to appearance, but judge with righteous judgment" (**John 7: 24**).

If you can be silent and watch your emotions and thoughts in those moments, you will come to see this ego face to face.

This ego will strongly pull out this nail of *"you need to be right"* and make all kind of suggestions to you. The followings are some examples of the suggestions:

Call this person and challenge him

Curse him out

How could you tolerate such a thing?

Your reputation is in danger
You are too weak

No one will respect you after this

You are too naïve

You are too gullible

People are judging you wrong, right now.

Once you witness these voices with no reaction, they will start going down. The law of nonresistance kills the voices of the ego. All you have to do is to breathe peacefully through the process by keeping your inhalation and exhalation at the same rhythm.

Only what you resist will persist, because resistance makes illusion real to the mind. However, there is something else you need to do, or these suggestions of the ego will resurface.

If you know that what is being said is true, then go deep inside and recognize that you are reaping a karmic return of your own thoughts and actions.

This is called claiming the power of your own creation back through critical self-analysis.

Go deep within and ask your heart to forgive you, God to release you from whatever you did, and ask that peace and harmony return in your consciousness and your universe.

If what is being said is not true, take enough time to bless everyone involved in the issue. The prayer should go this way:

Prayer

"I bless (name) with peace, love, harmony and truth."

You must do and repeat this blessing-prayer until all negative emotions leave your own heart, and then you can stop.

These are the two ways to recognize the truth in the center of your own being. There is no need for proving yourself right. Once you center yourself, all lies and all offenses vanish.

All you need is yourself and the truth at the center of your heart.

As you continue your practice, you will come to know a very deep stillness.

This stillness is greater than the normal peace that comes from the simple act of changing your thoughts. This stillness is the home of undisturbed tranquility. This stillness will reveal some amazing things to you.

It will reveal to you that you do not even need yourself, because you were never missing. You have always been there. You were simply unconscious of yourself.

It will also reveal to you that you did not even need the truth, because it was never missing. It has always been there.

It will reveal to you that you were never even offended. It was a lie.

Offense is an interpretation of someone else's reality by your own ego. Your true self knows only good and nothing else but good. In addition, your true identity which abides eternally in this stillness was not even aware that there was an offense.

The offense was the creation of your own mind or ego. Humans are artists, and they create an image of you in their own mind.

The gossips and insults were directed toward the image of you they have created in their own mind. It was never directed toward you. How can it be, since you are invisible all the time? No one has ever seen the real you.

You became angry and wanted to defend yourself, simply because yourself, you have become unconscious of YOU, and came to believe that you are the image in their mind.

Think about it. A purple light bulb can only project a purple light on the white wall. The blue light bulb can only project a blue light on the while wall. What the mind projects can only be in the mind and nowhere else.

People paint you upon the canvas of their own consciousness according to the way they perceive you in their own mind. They paint you with the colors of their own mind. You will always look the same to them. So, why bother defending yourself or trying to prove them wrong. Tomorrow, you will look the same to them again.

If the image people have created of you in their own mind was real, you should look the same to everyone and to yourself all the times. But you see yourself different. Other people see you different. So who has the real image? No one! You are a formless being. You are a Spirit.

Since the images of you are not real, to some you are nice, to some you are bad, to some you are good, to some you are ugly, to some you are fat, to some you look good, and so on; can you really keep up with these illusions? No, you can't.

So here, you are falling under the same trap of the ego, creating images for people in your mind, because you feel like you need to do so. This is what trying to make yourself right is all about.

Humans are artists. They draw your portrait on the white canvas of their own consciousness, by using their mental pencil (thoughts) and their own colors (emotions).

When you give them something they like, such as a gift, they paint you good. When you do something they do not like, they will destroy the old painting of you, and create another one that looks bad. Can you keep up with this? Is it even worth it?

Imagine you facing 100 artists who have all made a portrait of you, and you are going around trying to tear off all their canvases, because you do not like the portrait they made of you l. Do you see the insanity?

You cannot see the insanity. This is why you are trying to prove yourself right to others. Now that you see it, stop it. You want to prove yourself right to who? To who? To the artist? You cannot, because this is the way he sees you.

Wanting to be right is a foolish activity the ego binds your mind with, then goes on laughing at you, when you are hardly making insane and foolish attempt to change something that does not exist.

The truth is, when one of the artist changes his thoughts and feelings about you, you will look different on his canvas again and again and again. So how long will you be traveling this aimless road? Aren't you tired?

Leave the artists to their own works. Wanting to be right is trying to protect and keep an image of you. You can never keep the same image of you on everyone's canvas. There is no real need to do so. It is an illusion. You are imageless. If you die today, what image will you have? None!

People see your body, but they have never even seen you, because you are a Soul, invisible. How can anyone talk about what he cannot see? It is mind-made; an illusion. All images you have of yourself are born from your unconsciousness of who you are. Let go of them too. You are also an artist.

The only artist who will draw you well is the one who shows you a mirror to see yourself in it. This artist is no one else but your SELF. I call it inspiration. I call it God.

This mirror is the stillness within you that has no need to be known, to be liked, to be appreciated, or to be noticed for anything. That which is whole has none of these needs. The need to be right takes your unique beautiful right away from you, which is the right to be yourself.

Humans have turned all kinds of need into cultural exigencies. Humans cannot even serve freely and happily unless they are told, *"please"*. Even the need to hear the *"please"* before rendering an act of service or do something nice for another person is also from the ego who wants to be recognized or be begged before it does something.

Your authentic SELF is born with the heart to serve whether it is told *"please"* or not. The need to be right leads to this demand for *"please"* and *"thank you"*. The ego demands *thank you*, because it wants to be known for something.

If you want to serve a deaf and a mute person, what will you do? In that instant, your ego will justify the person as disabled and will not demand *thank you* or *please*. You see how ridiculous this is.

If we put the entire world on *"no please"* and *"no thank you"* diet, you will see how this world will go crazy. People will lose their mind.

When your true SELF gives, it gives selflessly. It waits for no reaction. It waits for no *"thank you's"*. It will not stop giving. It needs nothing. This is how the sun and Nature give.

If a *"thank you"* comes from the one who receives, your true SELF will kindly respond, *"You are welcome"*, but HE is not attached to it.

If the *"please"* comes, the true SELF is not attached to it either. If *"please"* is what makes you serve, then your service is from the ego. This is the truth. We call these behaviors *formulae for courtesy and ethical manners*, but in reality, they are not. They are from the ego.

People even gets hurt when they are not told *"please"* or *"Thank you"*. It is the same problem with you wanting people to tell you *"I am sorry"*.

People even wait for the *"I am sorry"*. It is the ego that seeks attention. The ego wants this in order to feel good, to feel important, and to feel superior. This is the reason it has the need to be right.

You already are peace. You already are the Self. You already are centered. Find your way back to YOU. End this game with the ego. Be awake!

What have you learned so far?

_____

_____

_____

_____

_____

_____

_____

_____

_____

_____

_____

_____

_____

_____

_____

_____

_____

_____

Sixth Nail

"You need help"

David sang, "I lift up my eyes to the mountains-- where does my help come from? My help comes from the LORD, the Maker of heaven and earth" (**Psalm 121: 1-2**). This Psalm really means, "I will raise my awareness to connect to God within, for where else will my help come from except from Him who makes the invisible become visible?"

True help is demanded through the sight of the Lord in all things and all people. It is the Spirit of the Lord or Love who gives to you through others all forms of help you may need. The ego can fake the need for help for attention and other means, because it does not see the Lord.

Yes, it is totally okay to ask for help. It is totally okay to receive help. It is totally okay to be suggested by others to seek help. There is nothing wrong with getting help. Yet, there is something wrong with our perception.

This sixth nail is a crafty one, in a sense that it has its own self-justification mechanism. It has power to justify its own weakness to get its way, yet the weakness is not real. It is a strategy it uses to force its will on others.

In the gospel, we saw the example of Martha and Mary. Martha was working hard in the kitchen to entertain Jesus. On the contrary, Mary was sitting with Jesus having a good time.

Suddenly, this ego of *"You need help"* spoke through Martha and said, *"Lord, I am working alone. Could you please ask Mary to help"*. Jesus, recognizing this voice replied, *"Mary has chosen the best way."* At this answer, the ego shrank and "shut up".

Mary and Martha did not know at that moment, that a spiritual deliverance took place. Yet, the ego knew that an energy of a very powerful frequency hit it through the words of Jesus. Martha was set free and spoke not after that.

The problem of this ego was not at all about the overbearing task in the kitchen. Not at all! I am telling you, not at all. The task was not at all overbearing. Its problem was that of jealousy. Yes! The ego in Martha believed that Mary was enjoying herself, which is what it also wanted. The ego was feeling like it was missing out on something very important. Therefore, it created the story of needing help.

This is how this ego acts all the times. Please, keep this in mind and make sure you always see it coming.

When you serve others with your whole heart, you amazingly attract grace from your superconscious mind to increase your strength. This strength is unusual. It is a divine stamina. It brings a very rare joy into your heart, and your body does not feel tired. You perform the service with inspiration. This strength is what this ego is after. It tricks you in going against your own grace.

In truth, you are not missing out on anything. Instead, you are gaining. When this ego speaks, whisper aggressively from your belly area, by exhaling these words out, *"My right is my own. My grace now comes. Everyone has chosen the best way."* This ego will vanish instantly after you repeat this with strong faith three times straight.

What have you learned so far?

_____

_____

_____

_____

_____

_____

_____

_____

_____

_____

_____

_____

_____

_____

_____

_____

_____

_____

_____

Seventh Nail

"You cannot do it without me"

The power of God is a treasure in the human soul. What can man do without God? Paul said, "But we have this treasure in jars of clay to show that this all-surpassing power is from God and not from us" (**2 Corinthians 4: 7**).

The seventh nail comes against you, when you make a decision to let go of fear. All nails of the ego feed on fear. The ego feels like it needs the belief that man is the body, because without this belief, it will come face to face with death. The fear of death is kept away through this false belief that one is the body.

Once you make the decision to let go of the material world, and live from the perspective that you are a spirit, you will hear this voice, *"You cannot do it without me"*. Suddenly, the things that you used to do will begin to appear hard to do.

The ego wants you to believe that you need it. The ego does not want to die. It does not want you to let it go, so it has to make you believe that without it your life will fall apart. This is a BIG lie. It's not true. It is by letting it go that you come to know LIFE as it really is, in its fullest expression as Love and bliss.

Jesus said to his disciples, "I am the vine; you are the branches. If you remain in me and I in you, you will bear much fruit; apart from me you can do nothing" (**John 15: 5**). You are always connected to your Divine Essence, the inner true vine of Eternal Life, Christ. You do not need the ego for survival.

When you make the decision to live by the above Truth, dramatic events will start happening. It will often time start with friends. The minute you choose to live for yourself, to be transparent, to tell the truth, to let people know how you are doing just as you are doing, the ego in your friends will start to feel threaten.

People who are close to you will suddenly start feeling as though you are letting them go or they are losing you. This is the proof that the ego likes to own. Their ego believed that it owned you.

Consequently, they will instantly notice the shift in your consciousness. They will know instantly, although you did not tell them anything. This is another proof that the spiritual world is real. It is beyond what we could even imagine.

The next thing is, they will start having attitude toward you. Believe me on this. It is going to be nasty. Because your own ego is dying, all the other egos around you will feel like you are killing them too. You will start losing friends over silly arguments. Family members will start reacting. This is the ego trying to make you believe that you cannot do it without it, that your life will become miserable.

Do not listen to its foolishness. These people will have to take their own journey to this place you are now stepping into.

You cannot be responsible for other people's journey of their own Self-discovery. Salvation is a sanctuary made for one soul at the time. They may not like the NEW YOU, because they do not know that whatever they have seen before, was never you, but the ego. Now that you are coming out as who you really are, they are running away from your presence; for they cannot stand the real "you".

They are not the ones running away. It is their ego. All of a sudden, all egos are afraid of you. They reason if you can kill one of them, you can kill all of them. People with strong egos will dislike you or try to be extra nice to you. These are signs of fear. They cannot tell why they are so uncomfortable with you. However, their egos know.

These egos are afraid to die. This is the ego on its defense when it senses you around. They are afraid to go to Golgotha. You become the cup of pain they want being removed from them.

Yet, there is no real escape for them. Your love will become painful to them. They cannot stand your smile. They cannot stand your happiness. Therefore, they will make a conscious decision not to believe that you are happy. Consequently, they will create a false belief that your happiness is fake and not real. This is the only way for them to keep their ego safe, and not fear death anytime you come around them.

To let this ego die, you will have to constantly affirm, *"It is in dying that I come to eternal Life. I am eternal and whole. I need nothing else, but ME"*

What have you learned so far?

_____

_____

_____

_____

_____

_____

_____

_____

_____

_____

_____

_____

_____

To have access to other books by This
Author, please visit www.onelifeone.com

THANK YOU!

Made in the USA
Charleston, SC
12 June 2014